Ornamental Design

An Image Archive for Artists & Designers

ELABORATE ORNAMENTAL DESIGN

Download Your Files

Downloading your files is simple. To access the download page, please go to the following url and enter your unique password. Please then follow the prompts to download your files.

Download Page:

www.vaulteditions.com/oda

Unique Password:

oda374hdt23

For technical assistance, please contact:

info@vaulteditions.com

Bibliographical Notes

This is a new work by Avenue house Press PTY LTD.

ISBN: 978-1-925968-22-4

Introduction

This title is the first volume in a series of comprehensive
and diverse pictorial archives of ornamental designs
for the practical use of artists and designers, or to be
appreciated by curious minds and botany enthusiasts.

This title features hundreds of exquisitely crafted 17th
and 18th-century etchings and engravings. This volume
features cartouches, sconces, pendants, frame designs,
Rocaille ornaments, scrolls, decorative arms and armour
motifs, elaborate portal designs, chinoiserie panels,
candelabras, floral motifs and much more.

With the aid of digital image editing technology, we
have been able to restore incredibly rare 17th-century
artwork into high-resolution images that are now
suitable for use in graphic design projects and many
other creative applications.

We hope you enjoy this resource.

01

ELABORATE ORNAMENTAL DESIGN

02

01. Various Designs for
Rocaille Ornamental
Frames.

02. Various Designs for
Rocaille Ornamental
Frames.

03

ELABORATE ORNAMENTAL DESIGN

03. Various Designs for
Rocaille Ornaments.

ELABORATE ORNAMENTAL DESIGN

04

05

04. Various Designs for
Rocaille Ornamental
Frames.

05. Various Designs for
Rocaille Ornamental
Frames.

06

07

ELABORATE ORNAMENTAL DESIGN

06. Various Designs for
Rocaille Ornaments.

07. Various Designs for
Rocaille Ornaments.

08

09

08. Design for a
Cartouche and
Representation of 'Sight'.

09. Design for a
Cartouche and
Representation of 'Smell'.

10. Design for a
Cartouche and a
Representation of 'Taste'.

11. Design for a Cartouche
and a Representation of
'Hearing'.

12

ELABORATE ORNAMENTAL DESIGN

13

12. Design for a
Cartouche.

13. Design for a
Cartouche.

14

ELABORATE ORNAMENTAL DESIGN

14. Design for a
Cartouche.

15

16

15. Design for a
Cartouche.

16. Design for a
Cartouche.

17. Design for a
Cartouche.

18. Banknote motifs—
six small lathe work
designs,

19

ELABORATE ORNAMENTAL DESIGN

20

19. Design for a
Cartouche.

20. Design for a
Cartouche.

21

ELABORATE ORNAMENTAL DESIGN

21. Design for a
Cartouche.

22

ELABORATE ORNAMENTAL DESIGN

22. Design for a
Cartouche.

23

23. Design for a
Cartouche.

ELABORATE ORNAMENTAL DESIGN

24. Design for a Rocaille
Cartouche with the Figure
of a Putto.

25. Design for a Rocaille
Cartouche with the Figure
of a Justitia.

26

ELABORATE ORNAMENTAL DESIGN

27

26. Design for a Rocaille
Cartouche with the Figure
of a Prudentia.

27. Design for a Rocaille
Cartouche with the Figure
of a Putto.

ELABORATE ORNAMENTAL DESIGN

28. Design for a large
Vase representing
'Earth'.

29. Design for a large
Asymmetrical Vase.

30. Design for a large
Vase representing
'Water'.

31. Design for a
large Vase or Ewer
representing 'Air'.

32

ELABORATE ORNAMENTAL DESIGN

32. Design for a large
Vase representing
'Fire'.

ELABORATE ORNAMENTAL DESIGN

33

34

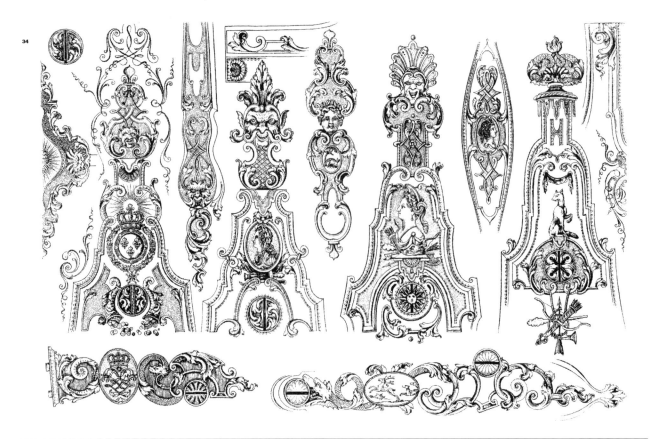

33. Plate seven from
Nouveavx Desseins
D'Arquebvseries.

34. Plate three from
Nouveavx Desseins
D'Arquebvseries.

35

De Lacollombe fecit

17 36

ELABORATE ORNAMENTAL DESIGN

35. Plate twelve from
Nouveavx Desseins
D'Arquebvseries.

ELABORATE ORNAMENTAL DESIGN

36. Plusievrs Pieces
et Ornements
Darquebuzerie.

37. Plusievrs Pieces
et Ornements
Darquebuzerie.

38

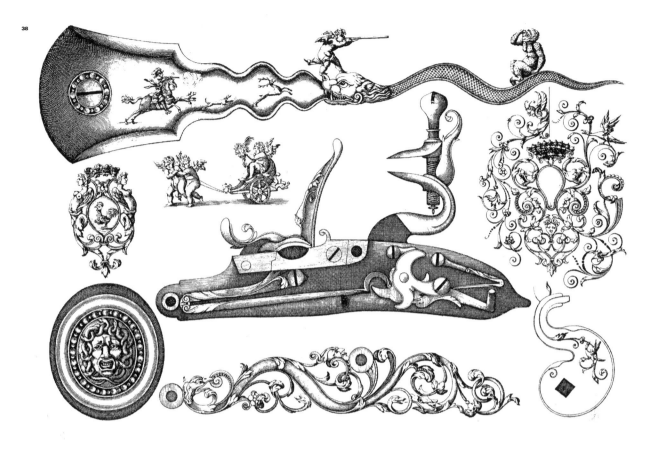

39

38. Plusievrs Pieces
et Ornements
Darquebuzerie.

39. Plusievrs Pieces
et Ornements
Darquebuzerie.

40

41

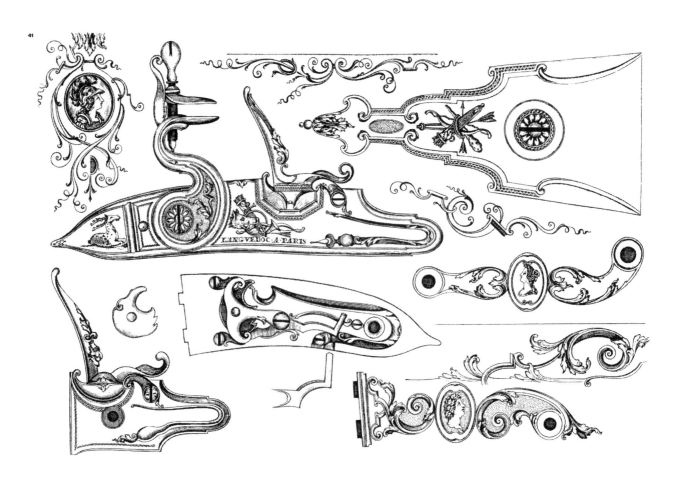

40. Plusievrs Pieces
et Ornements
Darquebuzerie.

41. Plusievrs Pieces
et Ornements
Darquebuzerie.

42. Plusievrs Pieces
et Ornements
Darquebuzerie.

43. Plusievrs Pieces
et Ornements
Darquebuzerie.

44

ELABORATE ORNAMENTAL DESIGN

45

44. Suggestions for
the Decoration of
Frames, Plate 4.

45. Suggestions for
the Decoration of
Frames, Plate 3.

46

47

ELABORATE ORNAMENTAL DESIGN

46. Suggestions for
the Decoration of a
door and window.

47. Suggestions for
the Decoration of a
door and window.

ELABORATE ORNAMENTAL DESIGN

48

49

48. Suggestions for
the Decoration of
Frames, Plate 4.

49. Suggestions for
the Decoration of
Frames, Plate 1.

50

51

ELABORATE ORNAMENTAL DESIGN

50. Suggestions for
the Decoration of
Frames, Plate 3.

51. Suggestions for
the Decoration of
Frames, Plate 2.

ELABORATE ORNAMENTAL DESIGN

52. Suggestions for
the Decoration of Altar
Frames, Plate 4.

53. Suggestions for
the Decoration of Altar
Frames, Plate 3.

54

55

ELABORATE ORNAMENTAL DESIGN

54. Suggestions for
the Decoration of Altar
Frames, Plate 2.

55. Suggestions for
the Decoration of Altar
Frames, Plate 1.

ELABORATE ORNAMENTAL DESIGN

56

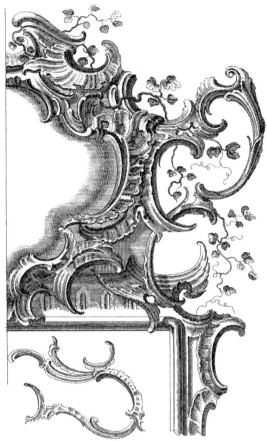

57

56. Suggestions for
the Decoration of
Frames, Plate 4.

57. Suggestions for
the Decoration of
Frames, Plate 3.

58. Suggestions for
the Decoration of
Frames, Plate 2.

59. Suggestions for
the Decoration of
Frames, Plate 1.

ELABORATE ORNAMENTAL DESIGN

60

62

61

63

60. Suggestion for
the Decoration of Top
Right Side of Portal.

61. Suggestion for
the Decoration of Top
Right Side of Portal.

62. Suggestion for
the Decoration of Top
Right Side of Portal.

63. Suggestion for
the Decoration of Top
Right Side of Portal.

64

ELABORATE ORNAMENTAL DESIGN

64. Various Designs for
Rocaille Ornaments.

ELABORATE ORNAMENTAL DESIGN

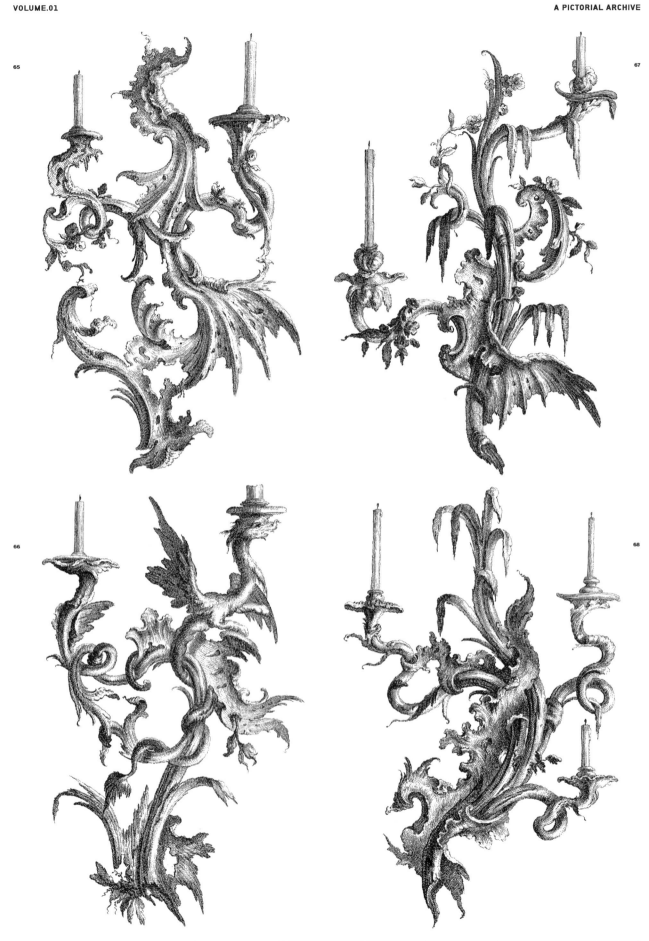

65. Design for a Two–Armed Candelabra, Plate 4.

66. Design for a Two–Armed Candelabra with a Dragon, Plate 1.

67. Design for a Two–Armed Candelabra with Rocaille Ornaments.

68. Design for a Three–Armed Candelabra, Plate 2.

69

69. Perspective view of
candelabrum.

70

ELABORATE ORNAMENTAL DESIGN

70. Ornaments Chinois (Bound
Collection of Chinoiserie
Panels) ca. 1765.

71

ELABORATE ORNAMENTAL DESIGN

71. Ornaments Chinois
(Bound Collection of
Chinoiserie Panels) ca. 1765.

72

72. Ornaments Chinois (Bound
Collection of Chinoiserie
Panels) ca. 1765.

73

ELABORATE ORNAMENTAL DESIGN

73. Ornaments Chinois
(Bound Collection of
Chinoiserie Panels) ca. 1765.

74

ELABORATE ORNAMENTAL DESIGN

74. Ornaments Chinois (Bound
Collection of Chinoiserie
Panels) ca. 1765.

75

ELABORATE ORNAMENTAL DESIGN

75. Ornaments Chinois
(Bound Collection of
Chinoiserie Panels) ca. 1765.

76

ELABORATE ORNAMENTAL DESIGN

F. Vivares Delin fecit

76. Ornaments Chinois (Bound
Collection of Chinoiserie
Panels) ca. 1765.

77

ELABORATE ORNAMENTAL DESIGN

77. Ornaments Chinois
(Bound Collection of
Chinoiserie Panels) ca. 1765.

ELABORATE ORNAMENTAL DESIGN

78

79

80

78. Ornaments Chinois
(Bound Collection of
Chinoiserie Panels).

79. Ornaments Chinois
(Bound Collection of
Chinoiserie Panels).

80. Ornaments Chinois
(Bound Collection of
Chinoiserie Panels).

81

ELABORATE ORNAMENTAL DESIGN

81. Ornaments Chinois
(Bound Collection of
Chinoiserie Panels) ca. 1765.

ELABORATE ORNAMENTAL DESIGN

82. Diverses Pieces de
Serruriers.

83. Diverses Pieces de
Serruriers.

84. Diverses Pieces de
Serruriers.

85. Diverses Pieces de
Serruriers.

ELABORATE ORNAMENTAL DESIGN

86. Diverses Pieces de Serruriers.

87. Diverses Pieces de Serruriers.

88. Diverses Pieces de Serruriers.

89

ELABORATE ORNAMENTAL DESIGN

89. A Sconce.

90

ELABORATE ORNAMENTAL DESIGN

90. A Sconce.

91

91. A Sconce.

92

ELABORATE ORNAMENTAL DESIGN

92. A Sconce.

93

93. A Sconce.

94

ELABORATE ORNAMENTAL DESIGN

94. A Sconce.

95

96

95. A Cartouche
Design.

96. A Cartouche
Design.

97

ELABORATE ORNAMENTAL DESIGN

97. A Cartouche
Design.

95

ELABORATE ORNAMENTAL DESIGN

98. A Cartouche
Design.

99

99. A Cartouche
Design.

ELABORATE ORNAMENTAL DESIGN

100. Two Designs for
Ceiling Decorations.

101. Two Designs for
Ceiling Decorations.

ELABORATE ORNAMENTAL DESIGN

102. Design for a
Ceiling Decoration.

103. Design for a
Ceiling Decoration.

104

105

104. Design for a
Ceiling Decoration.

105. Design for a
Ceiling Decoration.

106

107

ELABORATE ORNAMENTAL DESIGN

106. Design for a
Ceiling Decoration.

107. Design for a
Ceiling Decoration.

ELABORATE ORNAMENTAL DESIGN

108. Diverses Pieces
de Serruriers.

ELABORATE ORNAMENTAL DESIGN

109. Diverses Pieces
de Serruriers.

ELABORATE ORNAMENTAL DESIGN

110. Design for a
Pulpit.

111. Design for a
Pulpit.

112. Design for a
Pulpit

113. Design for the
Base of a Crucifix.

114

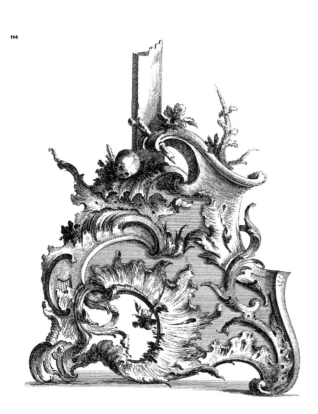

116

115

117

114. Design for the
Base of a Crucifix.

115. Design for a
Tabernacle.

116. Design for the
Base of a Crucifix.

117. Design for a
Confessional.

ELABORATE ORNAMENTAL DESIGN

118. Design for a
Tabernacle.

119. Design for a
Console Table.

120. Design for a
Tabernacle.

121

ELABORATE ORNAMENTAL DESIGN

121 Diverses Pieces
de Serruriers, title
page (recto).

ELABORATE ORNAMENTAL DESIGN

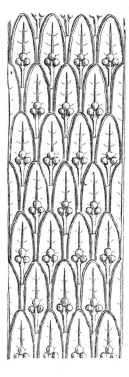

122. Illustrated Tariff
of Papier–Mâché
Picture Frames.

123. Illustrated Tariff
of Papier–Mâché
Picture Frames.

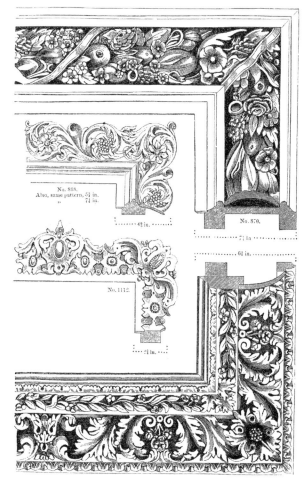

124. Illustrated Tariff
of Papier–Mâché
Picture Frames.

125. Plusievrs
Pieces et Ornements
Darquebuzerie.

126. Illustrated Tariff
of Papier–Mâché
Picture Frames.

127

ELABORATE ORNAMENTAL DESIGN

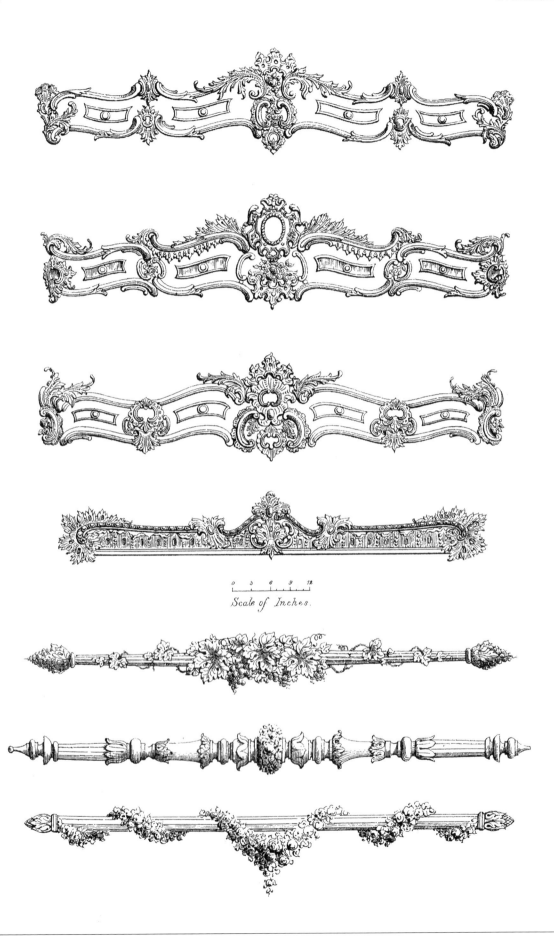

Scale of Inches.

127. Illustrated Tariff
of Papier–Mâché
Picture Frames.

128

ELABORATE ORNAMENTAL DESIGN

128. Illustrated Tariff
of Papier—Mâché
Picture Frames.

129

CCCLXXI.

129. Portrait of the Duke of
Northumberland, Vase and
Ornamental Frame.

130. Series of Small
Flower Motifs.

131. Series of Small
Flower Motifs.

132. Series of Small
Flower Motifs.

133

ELABORATE ORNAMENTAL DESIGN

133. Blackwork Design
for Broochs, Bracelets
and Pendants.

134

ELABORATE ORNAMENTAL DESIGN

134. Design for a
Pendant with Cupid.

ELABORATE ORNAMENTAL DESIGN

135

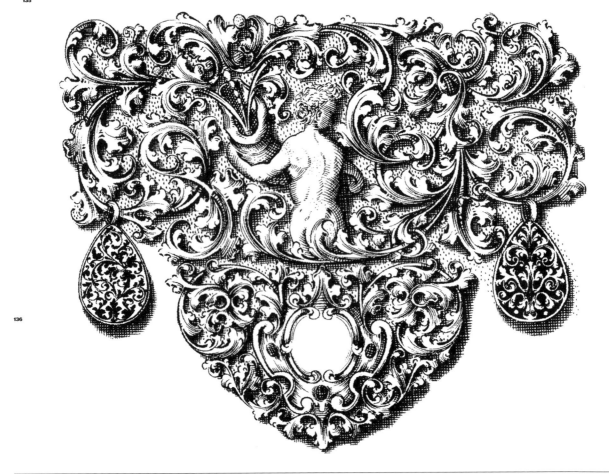

136

135. Gold work design.

136. Goldsmiths Ornament with a Young Man Holding a Cornucopia.

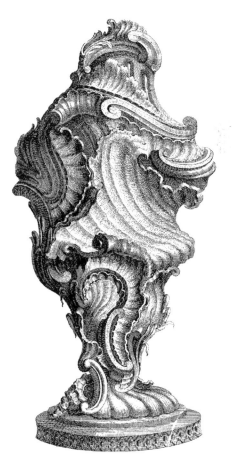

ELABORATE ORNAMENTAL DESIGN

137. Designs for a
Ewer and a Lidded
Vase.

138. Designs for Two
Lidded Vases.

Learn
More

Dicover more information about our pictorial

archive series at www.vaulteditions.com

For all technical queries regarding downloading

your assets, please contact:

info@vaulteditions.com

EDITIONS Vault

Printed in Poland
by Amazon Fulfillment
Poland Sp. z o.o., Wrocław

24524546R00047